SPOOKY

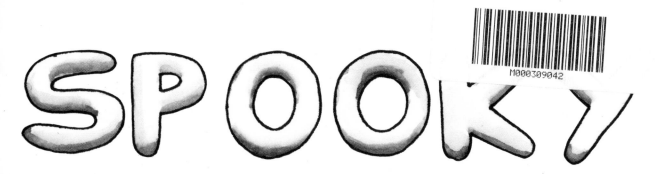

Jokes & Riddles

Written & Illustrated by Jeffrey S. Nelsen

Published by Checkerboard Press, a division of Macmillan, Inc.
CHECKERBOARD PRESS and colophon are trademarks of Macmillan, Inc.

ISBN 002-689070-4

Why did the skeleton go to bed early?
He was bone tired.

Knock knock!
Who's there?
Goblin.
Goblin who?
Goblin your food'll give you a tummy ache!

Who works on a ghost ship?
A skeleton crew.

3

How do you make points in monster soccer?
By kicking ghouls. (goals)

What happened when Dracula got mad?
He blew a casket. (gasket)

Why did the little girl
flunk witches' school?
She couldn't spell.

What do you call
a ghost hairdresser?
A boo-tician. (beautician)

What's a ghost's favorite game?
Hide-and-shriek.

What do vampires do on a date?
They go out for a bite.

5

What do you learn in ghoul school?
Reeling, Writhing, 'n' Bone-rattling.

What do you call a zombie with a bell?
A dead ringer.

What do you call a ghost auction?
Pick-a-boo.

7

Knock knock.
Who's there?
Coffin.
Coffin who?
Coffin without covering your mouth is bad manners.

What kind of music do ghosts write?
Sheet music.

9

Why aren't mummies fun at parties?
They're always speaking in "grave" voices.

What are a ghost and a zombie when they go on a date?

A boo-friend and a ghoul-friend.

What do witches call a party where everyone's too scared to have fun?
A success.

Why don't ghosts have jobs?
They're always making boo-boos.

What do you call a witch on the beach?
A sand-witch.

What does a ghost need
if he wants to scare people
in another state?

A haunting license.

What game are you playing
when you poke at ghosts
with a needle?

Prick-a-boo.

What do ghosts of pirates like to do?
Have a treasure haunt.

What does a baby ghoul play with?
A death rattle.

How did the prince feel when the witch
turned him into a frog?
He was hopping mad.

GRRRR RIBBET!!

How do you cheer up a haunted house?
Raise its spirits.

How do ghosts communicate?
On a ghost-to-ghost hookup.

What's a skeleton's favorite instrument?
A trom-bone.

What do skeletons do before they take a test?
They bone up.

Why do ghosts make good jazz musicians?
They have a lot of soul.

What happens when you cross
a witch and a wasp?

You get a "spell"-ing bee.

What do you call a skeleton
who doesn't like to work?

Lazy-bones.

What do you call
2,000 pounds of bones?

A skele-TON.

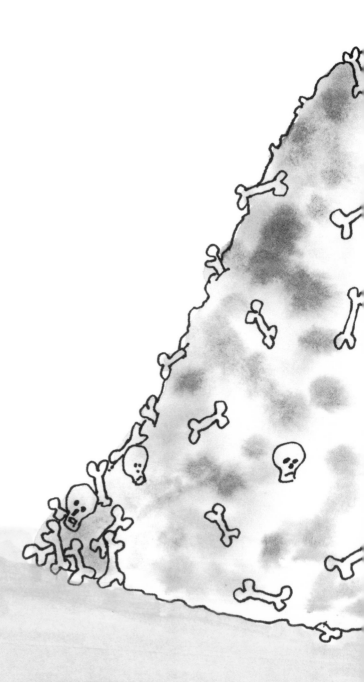

Where do students in witch school keep their notes?

In spell-binders.

How does a witch send messages?
By Hex-press Mail.

What does every witch parent try to be?
A good hex-ample.

What does a vampire take for a sore throat?
Coffin drops.

What did one skeleton say
to the other skeleton?
"If we had any guts
we'd get out of here."

Did you hear about the witch
who could hex people
into unconsciousness?
She had a fainting spell.

How do ghouls greet each other when they wake up?

"Good moaning to you!" (morning)

How do skeletons get to class?

They ride on the skull bus.

What do you get when you cross a duck with a grave?

An earth-quack. (earthquake)

Why are skeletons bad at school?

They're all bone-heads.

R.I.P. Elementary

Skull Bus

Do zombies eat cake with their fingers?
No. They eat the cake first,
THEN they eat their fingers.

Why do zombies have such good aim?
Because they always go for dead center.

What do you call a ghost
that runs through the jungle
with a machine gun?
Ram-boo.

Where does a haunted ship go?
Up and down the sea-ghost. (sea coast)

What do you call a sick ghost?
A haunting malady. (melody)

What's a vampire's favorite candy?
A sucker.

What do you call a dumb witch?
A nit-witch.

What kind of bees sting ghosts?
Boo-bees.

What are witches' adventures?
Hex-capades.

What is a witch after she casts
500 spells in one day?
Hex-hausted.

What do little ghouls have for breakfast?
Post Ghosties.

What do you call an army of vampires?
A bat-talion.

If a vampire gets promoted from sergeant,
what does he become?
A corpuscle. (corporal)